ISAAC ASIMOV'S NEW LIBRARY OF THE UNIVERSE

A DISTANT PUZZLE:
THE PLANET URANUS

BY ISAAC ASIMOV
WITH REVISIONS AND UPDATING BY FRANCIS REDDY

Gareth Stevens Publishing
MILWAUKEE

For a free color catalog describing Gareth Stevens' list of high-quality books, call 1-800-542-2595 (USA) or 1-800-461-9120 (Canada). Gareth Stevens' Fax: (414) 225-0377.

A special thanks to Evora Simien at the Jet Propulsion Laboratory and to Jody Swann and Kathy Teague at the United States Geological Survey.

Library of Congress Cataloging-in-Publication Data

Asimov, Isaac.
  A distant puzzle: the planet Uranus / by Isaac Asimov and Francis Reddy.
    p. cm. — (Isaac Asimov's New library of the universe)
  Rev. ed. of: Uranus: the sideways planet. 1988.
  Includes index.
  ISBN 0-8368-1136-4
  1. Uranus (Planet)—Juvenile literature. [1. Uranus (Planet)
  2. Planets.] I. Reddy, Francis, 1959-. II. Asimov, Isaac.
  Uranus: the sideways planet. III. Title. IV. Series:
  Asimov, Isaac. New library of the universe.
  QB681.A85   1994
  523.4'7—dc20   94-15424

This edition first published in 1994 by
Gareth Stevens Publishing
1555 North RiverCenter Drive, Suite 201
Milwaukee, Wisconsin 53212, USA

Project editor: Barbara J. Behm
Design adaptation: Helene Feider
Production director: Susan Ashley
Editorial assistant: Diane Laska
Picture research: Kathy Keller
Artwork commissioning: Kathy Keller and Laurie Shock

Printed in the United States of America

1 2 3 4 5 6 7 8 9 99 98 97 96 95 94

To bring this classic of young people's information up to date, the editors at Gareth Stevens Publishing have selected two noted science authors, Greg Walz-Chojnacki and Francis Reddy. Walz-Chojnacki and Reddy coauthored the recent book *Celestial Delights: The Best Astronomical Events Through 2001.*

Walz-Chojnacki is also the author of the book *Comet: The Story Behind Halley's Comet* and various articles about the space program. He was an editor of *Odyssey,* an astronomy and space technology magazine for young people, for eleven years.

Reddy is the author of nine books, including *Halley's Comet, Children's Atlas of the Universe, Children's Atlas of Earth Through Time,* and *Children's Atlas of Native Americans,* plus numerous articles. He was an editor of *Astronomy* magazine for several years.

CONTENTS

We live in an enormously large place – the Universe. It's only in the last fifty-five years or so that we've found out how large it probably is. It's only natural that we would want to understand the place in which we live, so scientists have developed instruments – such as radio telescopes, satellites, probes, and many more – that have told us far more about the Universe than could possibly be imagined.

We have seen planets up close. We have learned about quasars and pulsars, black holes, and supernovas. We have gathered amazing data about how the Universe may have come into being and how it may end. Nothing could be more astonishing.

We have learned a great deal, for instance, about a planet that is more than one and a half billion miles (two and a half billion kilometers) away from us. This planet is Uranus, which was named for the Greek god of the sky. Before 1986, we could only see it as a tiny spot of light through our telescopes. Now we have seen it up close and know much more about it and about the moons that circle it.

Isaac Asimov

A Modern-Day Planet

The year: 1781. The place: England. The event:
A German astronomer named William Herschel
studies the sky with a telescope he built himself.
On March 13, he sees a little spot of light where
no such spot should be. He thinks it must be a
comet, but it isn't fuzzy looking as comets
usually are. It moves slowly, night by night.
Herschel soon realizes that it is circling the Sun
far beyond the most distant planet then known –
Saturn. Herschel realizes he has discovered a
new, still more distant planet. All the other
planets have been known since ancient times.
This new planet is the first one to be discovered
in modern times. Its name: Uranus.

Opposite: On January 25,
1986, *Voyager 2* took this
photograph of Uranus from
a distance of 622,400 miles
(1 million kilometers). On this
journey, *Voyager* discovered
Uranus's additional rings and
ten new moons.

Top: Herschel's 40-foot (12-
meter) telescope was once the
largest in the world.

Bottom: Sir William Herschel,
holding a pamphlet announcing
his discovery of Uranus.

Discovery in Motion

What have we learned about this modern planet? Well, even without the help of the *Voyager 2* space probe, astronomers could determine some facts about Uranus by watching its motion. It is 1,800,000,000 miles (2,880,000,000 km) from the Sun. That is nineteen times as far from the Sun as Earth is. From the width of the planet at that distance, its true size can be determined. It is 31,765 miles (51,118 km) in diameter, which is four times the diameter of Earth. Uranus has a mass nearly fifteen times that of Earth, making it a giant planet. It is not nearly as large as Jupiter, though. Jupiter, the largest planet, is over twenty times as massive as Uranus.

! Bode's Law: too good to be true!

In 1772, the astronomer Daniel Titius developed a simple formula that showed how far each planet ought to be from the Sun. Another astronomer, Johann Bode, thought the formula was important and called it to everyone's attention. It was named "Bode's Law" for that reason. Using Bode's Law, a planet beyond Saturn ought to be about 1,800,000,000 miles (2,880,000,000 km) from the Sun. When Uranus was discovered in 1781, that proved to be its distance from the Sun! However, when Neptune, the next farthest planet, was discovered, it didn't fit Bode's Law. For that reason, astronomers stopped using the law.

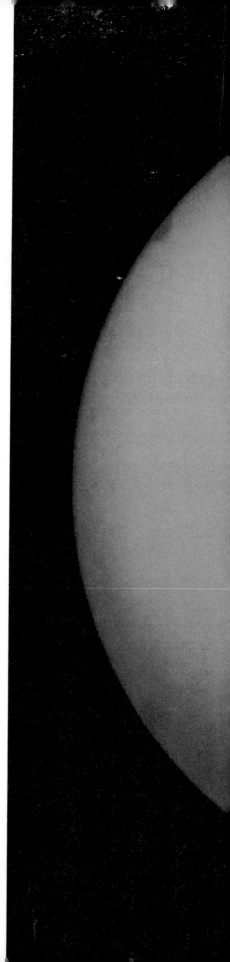

Right: Special color filters on *Voyager 2*'s cameras show the hazes produced by gases around the planet Uranus.

The Sideways Planet

Uranus is so far away that for about two hundred years, scientists could not determine how quickly it turns on its axis. They could tell there was something odd about the turning, though. Most planets turn on their axes in such a way that they are almost upright as they move around the Sun. Earth's axis is tipped only one-fourth of the way from the vertical. Uranus's axis, however, is tipped so far that it seems to be lying on its side as it moves around the Sun. It is the only planet with an axis tipped that way, making some people think of it as the "sideways planet."

Top: Small, solid particles, called planetesimals, may have existed at an early time in our Solar System. These could have collided with a newly formed planet, affecting the planet's tilt. Here, two planetesimals collide and fragment into smaller planetesimals.

Bottom: Uranus is known as the sideways planet since it rotates nearly 90° from the vertical. Earth, as you can see, is only slightly tilted in its rotation.

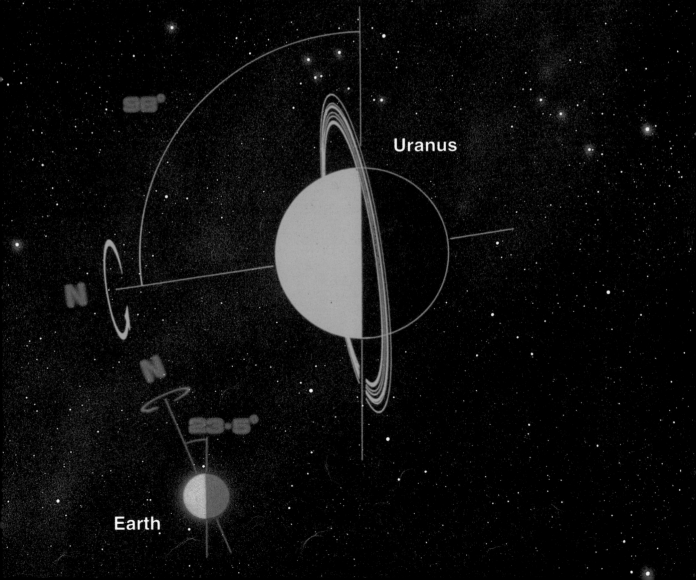

Uranus

Earth

Literary Moons

Like most planets, Uranus has its own natural satellites, or moons. These are smaller worlds that circle Uranus — just as our Moon circles Earth. Two were discovered by Herschel in 1787. He named them Oberon and Titania, after the king and queen of fairies in one of William Shakespeare's plays. Two more moons were discovered sixty-four years later. They were named Ariel and Umbriel, after two other fairies in a poem by Alexander Pope.

In 1948, a fifth satellite was discovered orbiting Uranus and was named Miranda, after a heroine in another of Shakespeare's plays. All these moons' orbits are tipped just as the planet's axis is. From Earth, the moons seem to go up and down, not side to side, like other planets' moons.

Introducing . . . the planet Herschel?

When Uranus was discovered, Herschel wanted to call it Georgium Sidus (Latin for "George's Star") in honor of George III, the British king. Other British astronomers wanted to call it Herschel in honor of its discoverer. Here is how astronomers finally named the planet: Beyond Earth, there is Mars. Then there is Jupiter, who is Mars's father in mythology; then Saturn, who is Jupiter's father. So they called the new planet Uranus, after Saturn's father.

Far left: The major moons of Uranus in sideways orbit around their parent planet. From outermost to closest, they are: Oberon, Titania, Umbriel, Ariel, and Miranda. Note how their orbits parallel, not only each other, but, Uranus's rings.

Left: A "family portrait" of the largest Uranian moons. From top to bottom: Miranda, Ariel, Umbriel, Titania, and Oberon. They are all named after characters in English literature. This composite photo shows how big these satellites are in relation to one another. Titania and Oberon are the largest and nearly the same size. Titania is 994 miles (1,600 km) in diameter; Oberon is 963 miles (1,550 km) in diameter.

Another World with Rings

In 1977, Uranus moved in front of a star. Astronomers watched closely because they wanted to measure how the starlight dimmed as Uranus's atmosphere passed in front of it. That would tell them something about the atmosphere. To their surprise, the star "blinked out" several times *before* the atmosphere moved in front of it. And it "blinked out" again several more times after Uranus and its atmosphere had moved away. From this, scientists determined that Uranus has rings circling it, just like Saturn. Saturn's rings are huge and bright, but Uranus's rings are very thin and dark.

! *The quiet giant*

All the planets known from ancient times are bright and move in the sky from one night to the next. But Uranus is much farther away, and, therefore, it is much dimmer. It also moves more slowly than the other planets. In 1690, an English astronomer, John Flamsteed, saw a dim star in the constellation Taurus. He called it 34 Tauri and marked it on his map. It was actually Uranus. If Flamsteed had gone back to look at it a few nights later, he would have noticed that it had moved. So you see, Uranus was actually seen ninety-one years before it was discovered.

Right: Like Saturn's rings, the rings of Uranus are not solid. Instead, they are made of millions of chunks of rocky ice.

Inset: The dark ring system of Uranus shows up best when lit from behind, but such a view is impossible from Earth. The *Voyager 2* spacecraft took this picture of the rings when it raced past Uranus in 1986. The ring system consists of ten narrow rings of rock or ice particles, a broad ring of dust, and dozens of dusty ringlets.

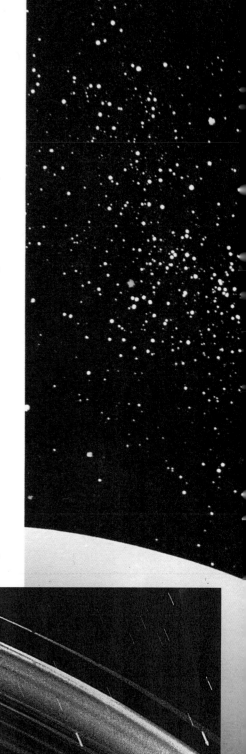

A Challenging Planet

Astronomers were excited by the surprising discovery of rings around Uranus. But it didn't seem as though they would ever find out more information about Uranus. It was so far away that it just looked like a little bluish circle of light. Jupiter and Saturn, two planets that are closer and larger than Uranus, can be seen much more easily. In fact, these two giants appear so clearly in telescopes that markings on the surfaces can be seen. The markings move over the surfaces, and we can see how fast these planets rotate. But Uranus, small and dim, does not show markings. This has puzzled scientists for over two hundred years.

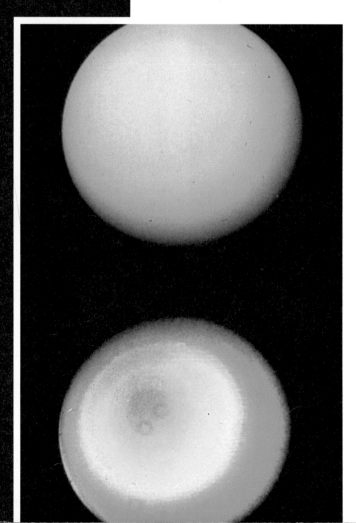

Left: Closing in on Uranus: This photo of Uranus was taken by *Voyager 2* from 153 million miles (247 million km) away, on July 15, 1985 — six months before the January, 1986, flyby. This was the first real chance for scientists to see the relation of the planet to its moons. In this composite picture, several of the moons can be seen.

Inset: Two views of Uranus: The top picture shows how the planet would appear to a person in a spacecraft 11 million miles (18 million km) from Uranus. The other picture is taken through color filters and enhanced by computer to show the gases present on and around Uranus. In both shots, the view is toward the planet's pole of rotation, which lies just left of center.

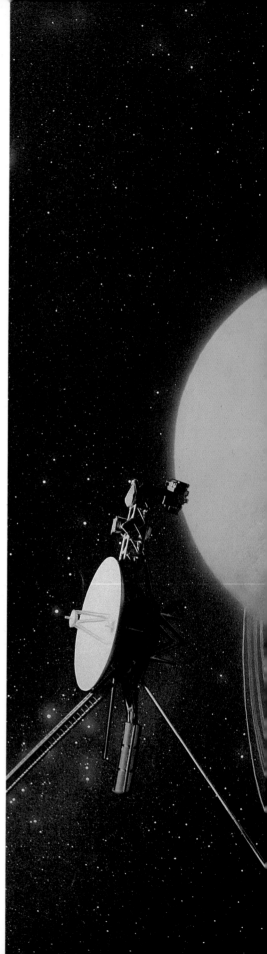

Top and right: Voyager 2 came closest to Uranus on January 24, 1986. Some of the photographs in this book were taken on that mission. After photographing Uranus, *Voyager 2* headed for its 1989 look at Neptune.

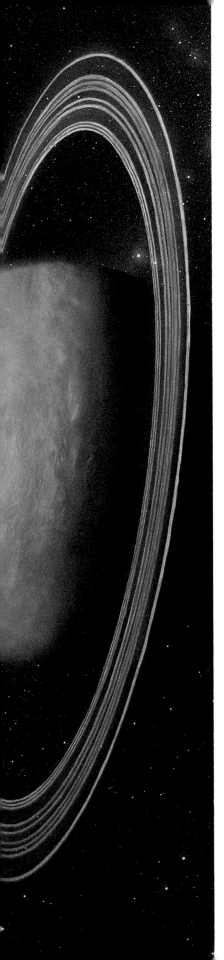

Probing the Planet

Today, we have learned far more about Uranus than we knew even as recently as the early 1980s — and in ways that astronomers like Herschel might not even have imagined. We have built space probes, and they have traveled to the distant planets. *Voyager 1* and *Voyager 2* were sent into space in 1977. Both *Voyager* probes passed Jupiter and Saturn, taking photographs as they flew by. *Voyager 2* had its course arranged so that it continued toward Uranus. It passed Uranus in January, 1986, and photographed it. This wasn't easy, because Uranus is so far from the Sun that it only gets 1/360 as much light as we do. *Voyager 2* had to take pictures in this dim light as it was moving past, but it did a magnificent job.

And now that *Voyager 2* has flown past Uranus, we know much more about this giant planet. For example, we now know that Uranus may have a molten rock core that is 8,000 miles (13,000 km) in diameter. This is about the size of Earth. This core is surrounded by a 5,000-mile- (8,000-km) deep "sea" made of mostly water, and a 7,000-mile- (11,000-km) thick atmosphere of helium and hydrogen. With so much of the planet made up of a gaseous atmosphere, Uranus is one of the gas giants — joining a group that includes Jupiter, Saturn, and Neptune.

Opposite, bottom: Landing on a gaseous planet like Uranus would be impossible since the planet really has no land. This cutaway picture shows the planet's three layers – a center of molten rock, surrounded by a layer of liquid and an outer layer of gas.

Important Clues

Voyager 2's photographs were beamed back to Earth. They showed Uranus much more clearly than we can see it with a telescope from Earth. However, it still turned out to be just a blue globe. Sunlight warms the atmospheres of Jupiter and Saturn, stirring the clouds into circles and belts. But Uranus receives so little sunlight that its atmosphere is much quieter. The *Voyager* scientists took special photos that revealed bright, thin clouds deep in the atmosphere of Uranus. Radio signals also showed that it takes Uranus about 16-3/4 hours to turn on its axis. Until then, guesses had been anywhere from 10 to 25 hours.

Scientists were delighted that they could now compare the motions of the clouds to Uranus's spin, since that information gives them important clues about the way weather works on Uranus.

Right: A Uranian cloud. This *Voyager 2* photograph shows a cloud along the bluish edge of Uranus. The photo was taken through color filters and enhanced by computer. In true color, the cloud would have been nearly invisible.

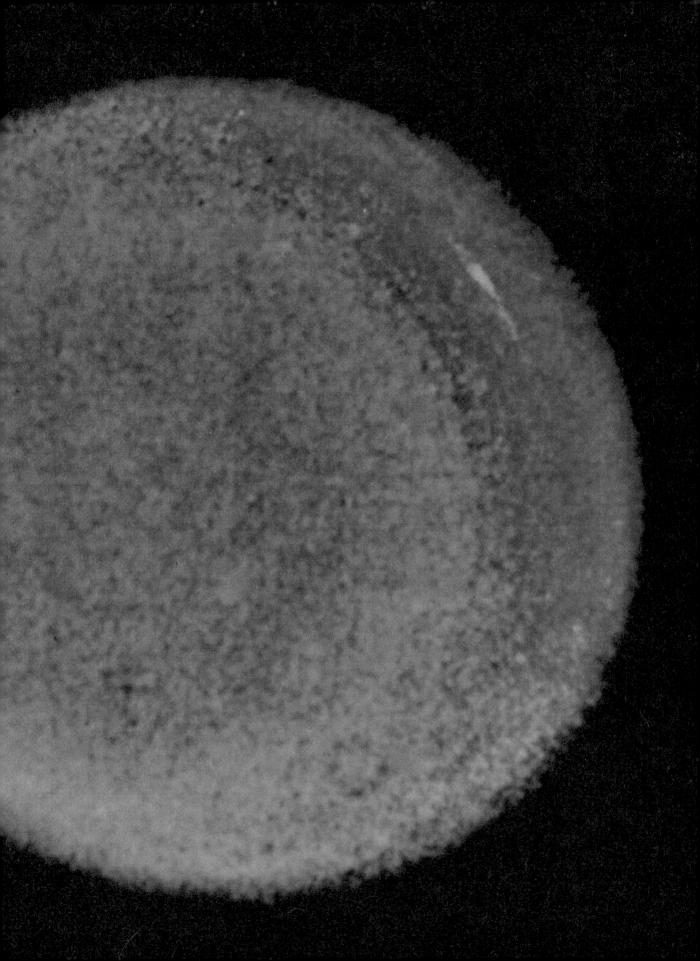

Moons and More Moons

We now know that Uranus has fifteen moons in all. Only five are large enough to be seen with telescopes from Earth. In 1986, *Voyager 2* discovered ten more moons. The smallest of these are only about 30 miles (50 km) in diameter. Like the particles in the rings, the small moons are all as dark as coal.

Umbriel is the darkest of the big moons. A bright circle stands out against its battered gray surface like a powdered doughnut on a dark plate. This may be caused by bright, clean ice dug up by a recent collision. Oberon, the moon farthest from Uranus, is 963 miles (1,550 km) across. A strange, dark material coats the floor of one of its craters. On the largest moon, Titania, a giant valley stretching over 994 miles (1,600 km) shows where its frozen crust split open long ago.

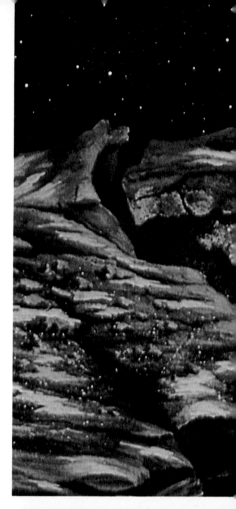

❓ *Why are Uranus's rings so dark?*

If the rings were composed of icy particles, they would reflect most of the light that falls on them and would glitter brightly. Instead, Uranus's rings seem to be made of dark material. Perhaps the rings began as a mixture of ice and rock, and the ice slowly evaporated, leaving the rock behind. But Saturn's bright rings haven't evaporated, and Saturn gets four times as much sunlight as Uranus. Perhaps the real mystery is why Saturn's rings are so bright.

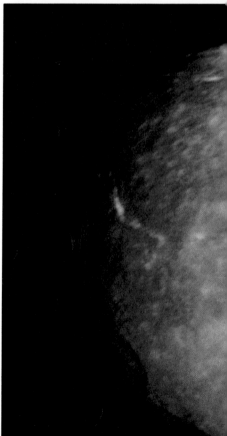

Top: Titania has fewer large craters than Oberon. Flows of ice and rock probably flooded Titania's oldest and largest craters when the moon was still young. Its surface expanded and cracked as it cooled, creating giant valleys hundreds of miles long (zigzag at left).

Right: Uranus as viewed from Titania, the second farthest of Uranus's five large moons.

Opposite, bottom: A dark mix of ice and rock oozed out of Oberon's interior to fill the crater near the center of this picture.

20

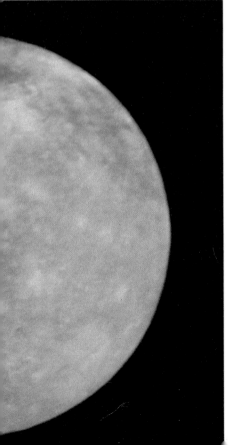

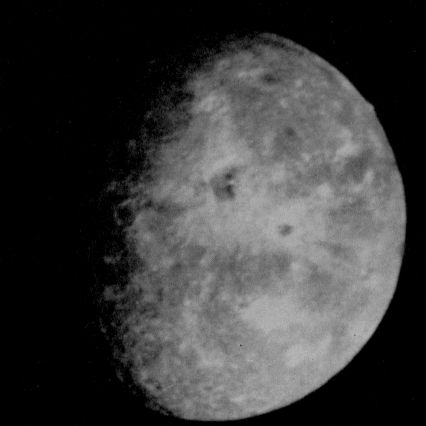

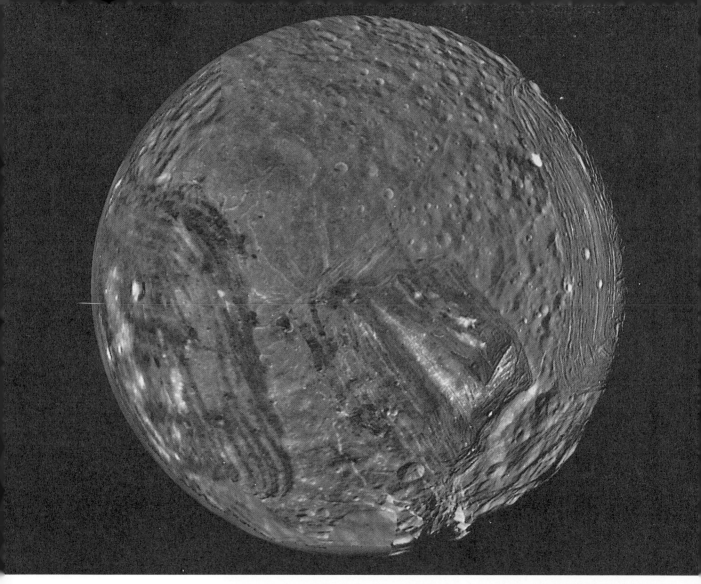

Cracked Worlds

Large craters pepper the faces of Umbriel, Oberon, and Titania, but few craters can be found on Ariel. Instead, there is a network of crisscrossing valleys. Scientists believe the valleys formed when Ariel's surface cooled, expanded, and cracked. Icy material — possibly frozen water and ammonia — then oozed out of the moon's cracks. It coated the valley floors, smoothed the surface, and buried many craters.

Miranda, a moon just 301 miles (484 km) in diameter, rates as one of the strangest worlds in the Solar System. Its surface has cratered plains, a deep valley, and unusual areas etched by curving grooves and ridges. Scientists think that, as this moon formed, rocky material began to sink toward its center, and icy material (the grooved regions) started to rise toward the surface. But tiny Miranda froze solid before this process was finished, leaving the jumbled world that *Voyager 2* photographed.

Opposite, top: Nine *Voyager 2* images were combined and processed by computer to create this portrait of Miranda. The bright cliffs of a valley much deeper than Earth's Grand Canyon are visible at the bottom; the moon's south pole is at the center.

Opposite, bottom: Miranda's terrain has grooves that could reach depths of a mile or more. One day, probes may discover important information about Uranus and its moons.

Below: This picture is a mosaic of images taken some 81,000 miles (130,330 km) from Ariel. Movements of rock and ice have reshaped the surface of this moon.

More Appealing Than We Think

With the *Voyager 2* flyby of 1986, Uranus earned a reputation for being the least appealing planet in the Solar System. Scientists expected Neptune to look much the same as Uranus — a colored gas ball with few if any clouds or storms visible. Yet when *Voyager 2* flew past Neptune in 1989, it found a stormy atmosphere. A storm the size of our entire Earth, dubbed the Great Dark Spot, could be seen on Neptune long before the spacecraft reached the planet. Closer in, wispy white clouds raced around the planet, driven by some of the fastest winds of any in the Solar System!

So why wasn't Uranus more like Neptune? Well, perhaps it is! In 1993, astronomers using Earth-based telescopes found a dark spot in the atmosphere of Uranus. Perhaps the weather on Uranus is more interesting than we think — and *Voyager 2* caught it during an inactive period.

Right: In 1989, *Voyager 2* observed the Great Dark Spot — a storm as large as Earth — and other cloud features in Neptune's atmosphere. A similar feature was recently found on Uranus.

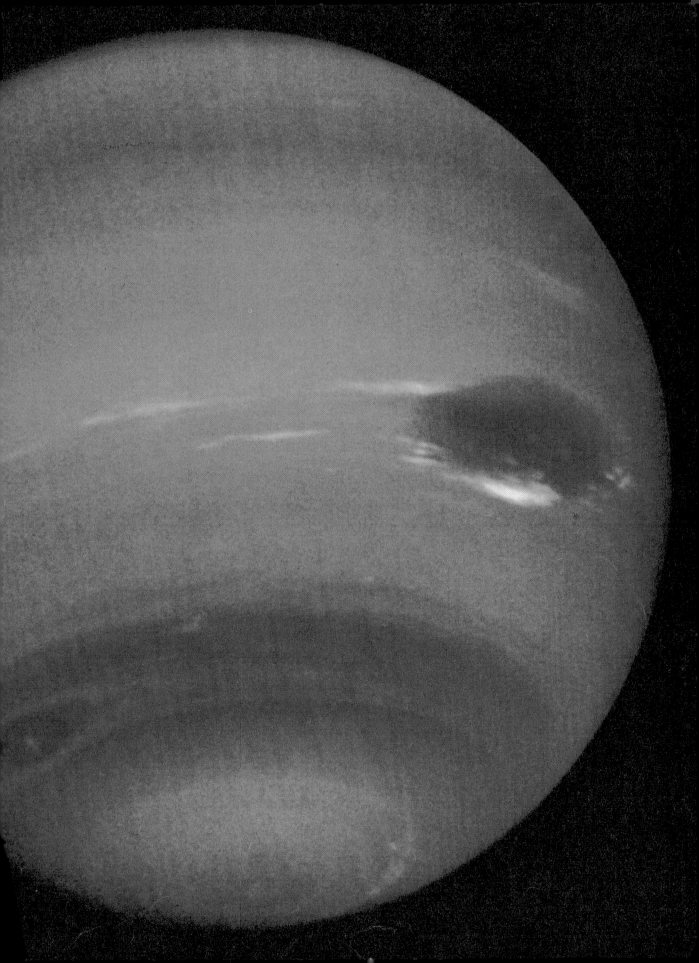

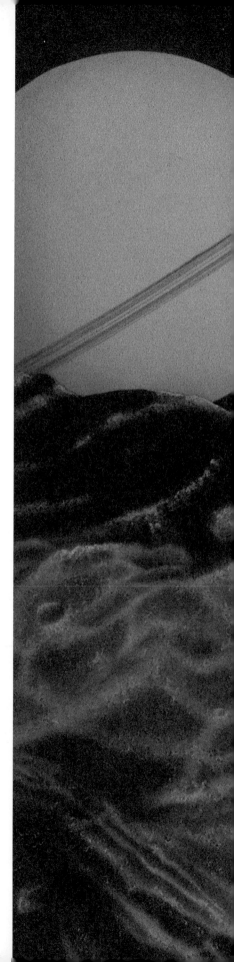

A Century Beyond

The pictures sent back by *Voyager 2* are all we have with which to study Uranus, its rings, and its satellites in detail. What's more, we will not have other pictures of this kind for a long time. It may be many years, perhaps even a century, before another probe is launched to study Uranus. Of course, by the time a hundred years passes, we will have more advanced probes that can study the planet in greater detail. Who knows? Perhaps the next probe will even carry humans with it!

❓ *Another planet to be discovered?*

When Uranus was first discovered, it didn't seem to follow exactly the law of gravity as it turned around the Sun. It seemed to lag a bit. Perhaps there was another large planet beyond it that had not yet been discovered. The gravitational pull of this more distant planet wasn't allowed for. If this were considered, it might account for Uranus's lag. Scientists looked for, found, and named Neptune. However, there is still a very small lag in Uranus's motion around the Sun that cannot be explained by the presence of either Neptune or tiny Pluto, which was discovered in 1930. Is there another large planet beyond Neptune? If so, it has not yet been found. If not, what causes that last bit of lag?

Right: Could this child be a future relative of yours? He or she could be one of the first to travel to Uranus.

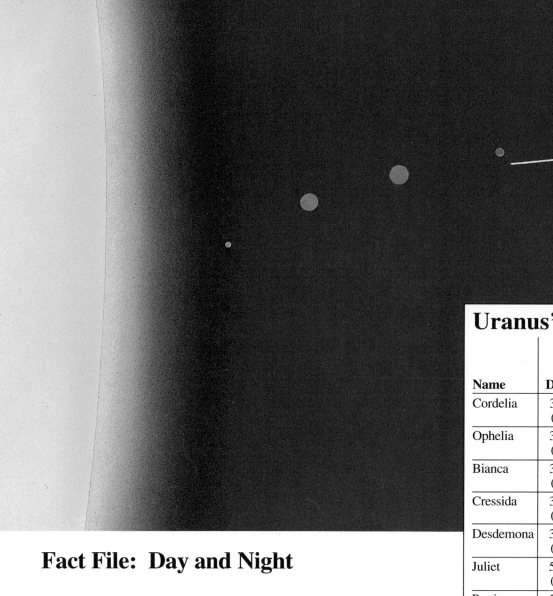

Fact File: Day and Night

Uranus, the third largest planet and the seventh farthest from the Sun, is also one of the most unusual. Its tipped axis means that each pole faces the Sun during half of Uranus's 84-year orbit. This means that each half of Uranus has a 42-year-long "day" of sunlight followed by a 42-year-long "night" of darkness.

Uranus's Satellites

Name	Diameter	Distance from Uranus's Center
Cordelia	31 miles (50 km)	30,915 miles (49,750 km)
Ophelia	31 miles (50 km)	33,406 miles (53,760 km)
Bianca	31 miles (50 km)	36,762 miles (59,160 km)
Cressida	37 miles (60 km)	38,384 miles (61,770 km)
Desdemona	37 miles (60 km)	38,937 miles (62,660 km)
Juliet	50 miles (80 km)	39,993 miles (64,360 km)
Portia	50 miles (80 km)	41,075 miles (66,100 km)
Rosalind	37 miles (60 km)	43,455 miles (69,930 km)
Belinda	37 miles (60 km)	46,767 miles (75,260 km)
Puck	106 miles (170 km)	53,447 miles (86,010 km)
Miranda	301 miles (484 km)	80,645 miles (129,780 km)
Ariel	721 miles (1,160 km)	118,837 miles (191,240 km)
Umbriel	740 miles (1,190 km)	165,274 miles (265,970 km)
Titania	994 miles (1,600 km)	270,831 miles (435,840 km)
Oberon	963 miles (1,550 km)	362,027 miles (582,600 km)

Above: The Sun and its Solar System, from left: Mercury, Venus, Earth, Mars, Jupiter, Saturn, Uranus, Neptune, and Pluto. *Right:* A close-up of Uranus and its five major satellites (*from top to bottom*): Miranda, Ariel, Umbriel, Titania, and Oberon. *Voyager* 2 has now found ten more moons.

Uranus versus Earth

Planet	Diameter	Rotation Period (length of day)	Period of Orbit around Sun (length of year)	Known Moons	Surface Gravity	Distance from Sun (nearest-farthest)	Least Time for Light to Travel to Earth
Uranus	31,765 miles (51,118 km)	17 hours, 5 minutes	30,685 days (84.01 years)	15	0.79*	1.7-1.9 billion miles (2.7-3 billion km)	2.5 hours
Earth	7,927 miles (12,756 km)	23 hours, 56.1 minutes	365.256 days (one year)	1	–	92-95 million miles (147-152 million km)	–

* Multiply your weight by this number to find out how much you would weigh on this planet.

More Books about Uranus

Exploring Outer Space: Rockets, Probes, and Satellites. Asimov (Gareth Stevens)
Our Planetary System. Asimov (Gareth Stevens)
Planets. Barrett (Franklin Watts)
The Planets. Couper (Franklin Watts)

Video

Uranus: The Sideways Planet. (Gareth Stevens)

Places to Visit

You can explore Uranus and other parts of the Universe without leaving Earth. Here are some museums and centers where you can find a variety of space exhibits.

Virginia Air and Space Center
600 Settlers Landing Road
Hampton, VA 23669

Lawrence Hall of Science
One Centennial Drive
Berkeley, CA 94720

Edmonton Space and Science Centre
11211-142nd Street
Edmonton, Alberta K5M 4A1

Ontario Science Centre
770 Don Mills Road
Don Mills, Ontario M3C 1T3

Henry Crown Science Center
Museum of Science and Industry
57th Street and Lake Shore Drive
Chicago, IL 60637

Hayden Planetarium
Museum of Science
Science Park
Boston, MA 02114-1099

Sydney Observatory
Observatory Hill
Sydney, NSW 2000 Australia

Australian Museum
6-8 College Street
Sydney, NSW 2000 Australia

Places to Write

Here are some places you can write for more information about Uranus. Be sure to state what kind of information you would like. Include your full name and address so they can write back to you.

National Space Society
922 Pennsylvania Avenue SE
Washington, D.C. 20003

NASA Kennedy Space Center
PA-ESB
Kennedy Space Center, FL 32899

The Planetary Society
65 North Catalina Avenue
Pasadena, CA 91106

Jet Propulsion Laboratory
Public Affairs 180-201
4800 Oak Grove Drive
Pasadena, CA 91109

Glossary

astronomer: a scientist who studies the worlds beyond our Earth, including the other planets, the stars, comets, and more.

atmosphere: the gases that surround a planet.

axis: the imaginary line through the center of a planet around which the planet rotates. The axis of Uranus is tilted so that the planet appears to be on its side compared to the other planets in our Solar System.

billion: the number represented by 1 followed by nine zeroes – 1,000,000,000. In some countries, this number is called "a thousand million." In these countries, one billion would then be represented by 1 followed by twelve zeroes – 1,000,000,000,000: a million million.

Bode's Law: a formula that showed how far each planet should be from our Sun. Daniel Titius developed this formula that later turned out to be false.

crater: a hole in the ground caused by a volcanic explosion or meteor strike.

diameter: a straight line across the center of a circle or sphere from one side to the other.

gas: a substance that is neither solid nor liquid.

gravity: the force that causes objects like planets and their moons to be attracted to one another.

helium: a light, colorless gas that, along with hydrogen, makes up the atmosphere of Uranus.

Herschel, William: a German astronomer who first discovered Uranus in 1781.

mass: a quantity, or amount, of matter.

natural satellites: another name for the moons that orbit planets.

planet: one of the bodies that revolves around our Sun. Our Earth is one of the planets as is Uranus.

planetesimals: small bits of matter that, when joined together, may have formed planets.

radio telescope: an instrument that uses a radio receiver and antenna to both see into space and listen for messages from space.

rings: bits of matter that circle some planets, including Uranus.

space probes: satellites that travel in space, photographing celestial bodies and even landing on some of them. *Voyager 1* and *Voyager 2* are probes.

Universe: everything that we know exists and believe may exist.

Uranus: a Greek god of the sky and the father of Saturn. The planet Uranus is named for him.

Voyager 2: the space probe that sent back to Earth valuable information about Uranus.

Index

Born in 1920, Isaac Asimov came to the United States as a young boy from his native Russia. As a young man, he was a student of biochemistry. In time, he became one of the most productive writers the world has ever known. His books cover a spectrum of topics, including science, history, language theory, fantasy, and science fiction. His brilliant imagination gained him the respect and admiration of adults and children alike. Sadly, Isaac Asimov died shortly after the publication of the first edition of *Isaac Asimov's Library of the Universe*.

The publishers wish to thank the following for permission to reproduce copyright material: front cover, © Julian Baum; 4, NASA; 4-5 (upper), Royal Astronomical Society; 4-5 (lower), National Maritime Museum; 6-7, NASA; 8-9 (upper), © David Hardy; 8-9 (lower), 10-11, © Julian Baum 1988; 11, NASA; 12, NASA/JPL; 12-13, © David Hardy; 14-15, NASA; 15, United States Geological Survey; 16 (upper), © Julian Baum 1986; 16 (lower), © Lynette Cook 1988; 16-17, © Julian Baum 1986; 18-19, United States Geological Survey; 20-21 (upper), © MariLynn Flynn 1982; 20-21 (lower), 21, NASA/JPL; 22 (upper), Frank Reddy; 22 (lower), © Alan Gutierrez 1979; 23, NASA; 24-25, NASA/JPL; 26-27, Courtesy of Spaceweek National Headquarters; 28-29 (all), © Sally Bensusen 1987.